NYS Court Officer Exam Review 2014

Seth S. Patton

ISBN: **1494935899**
ISBN-13: **978-1494935894**

DEDICATION

This book is dedicated to the memory of Andrew F. Judge, Jr. who served our state and city in the NYPD and as a NYS Court officer.

CONTENTS

DISCLAIMER

The author and this book have no relationship with the NYS Unified Court System

Chapter 1, The Last Court Officer Trainee Exam, 2009

My Thoughts and Recollections of the NYS Court Officer Exam

I took the 2009 exam at Forest Hills High School In Queens, New York. The building itself is a large, old high school. After checking in at the front desk, everybody was held in the auditorium. We were then sent into classrooms for the exam. The room was very warm near the windows and the radiator, but very cold near the door. It would have been helpful to dress in layers, so that I could have adjusted my clothing in order to be comfortable.

The school is in a residential area and parking would have been an issue had I not arrived early. I knew where the school was ahead of time, which helped lower my stress level.

Even though I applied to take the exam very soon after the posting was up, I was assigned the later of the two dates. Candidates were assigned dates somewhat randomly and there were numerous sites in Queens county alone.

The most remarkable part of the exam for me was the first section, "Remembering Facts and Information". It was necessary to read in such a way that I could imprint very specific information into my memory so that I could answer the following questions accurately.

This test also required me to read very carefully. It had many questions that were designed to trick a careless reader. There always seemed to be a fast, easy answer that was misleading. Success on this exam required me to read through an entire question, understand it fully, and respond with accuracy. I had to re-read several questions to find the correct answer.

What was also interesting about this exam is that, although topics and readings are about court scenarios, no prior knowledge of law or policy was required. All of the necessary information was given to me. My job in this exam was to read it carefully and respond accurately.

The exam had 60 questions and each one was worth 1.67%. Each question was multiple choice and had four possible answers to choose from. Even though I did very well on the exam, I was ranked 1817. This meant that 1816 people scored higher than or equal to my score, or claimed veteran's benefits. I was called in the first canvassing, about a year and a half following the exam. I also went for and passed my medical examination.

N.B. There is the opportunity to receive veteran's benefits on the exam which could add up to 10 points on your score. The trainee guide will contain updated service dates and details. **In order to claim this benefit, you must check the box on the application form.**

My medical examination was uneventful except for the hearing part. I was brought into a room and told to put on headphones. I was then instructed to raise my hand when I heard a tone. While this was going on, there was background noise coming from other parts of the office. This made it difficult to distinguish between the sounds outside and the hearing test. I should have informed the examiner of this, but I was able to get through the test OK.

My recommendation is to raise your hand if there is any chance you hear a sound- The examiner should not drop your score for false-positive responses. Also, if there is something not right, such as background noise or people talking, you should speak up politely, but firmly. You really don't have much recourse after the fact if the examiner makes an error against you.

Long before your medical examination you should check your weight and blood pressure against the charts published online in the trainee candidate manual. I was close to the weight limit and kept an eye on it during the weeks following up to the medical. If you need to drop serious weight or get your blood pressure under control, the more time you have to do it, the better.

I was all clear to move on to the physical ability assessment when another job opportunity came up, so I withdrew my candidacy. I later learned that the class I would have been in was called off just a few days before starting the academy due to a hiring freeze imposed by Governor Cuomo. Had I quit my job, bought my uniform and training gear, I would have been out of luck.

If all goes well for you on the examination and medical, you will complete the physical ability test and the background investigation. The activities outlined in the trainee website should provide you with a clear expectation of what physical activities you will need to master. You should start practicing early. You can also expect that these exercises will be similar to other law enforcement exams.

In terms of the background investigation, it would be wise to be prepared. First, request a NYS DMV drivers license abstract. If you have prior suspensions, or other issues, you will get a head start on identifying violations, dates and courts that you will need to provide to your investigator.

Also run your plates through any online parking violations and red light camera searches such as the one the NYC Department of Finance has. All outstanding summonses and warrants will need to be clear in advance.

If you have ever been arrested, it will be necessary to obtain a disposition from the court which is a statement explaining what the charge was and will give the result of any charges and cases.

If you served in the Armed Forces, you will also be required to have your discharge papers available.

Having all of this information available will help expedite your investigation, get you cleared faster, and make you eligible to start with the soonest possible class.

A final thought concerning the entire process is to provide a mailing address on all of your paperwork that is going to be good for several years. The process is slow, and the court officer recruitment office sends out materials that are very time-sensitive. They are not going to call you if you miss a deadline or appointment, they will simply make you inactive.

Chapter 2, Develop Your Study Plan

Schedule Your Study:

Find a regular time in your schedule when you can regularly devote a half an hour or more of quiet study time, free of distractions.

Set a schedule and stick to it. Discuss your schedule with your family so that everybody understands your need for uninterrupted study time.

Start practicing your memory skills in everyday life. If you are walking and see a billboard, take 10 seconds to look at it carefully. Then, as you go about your way, try to remember details such as color, names, and dates. If you ride the subway, there are numerous opportunities to practice this method because you have so many different advertisements to view.

Focus:

Study without distractions to the best of your ability. Turn off your phone. Inform people close to you that you will be unavailable during that time so that there is no expectation of a callback.

Be sure you are getting enough sleep, as this can greatly affect your concentration and memory skills. Creating a peaceful sleep environment by eliminating lights and sounds, obtaining quality pillows, and limiting nighttime activities can help. You should not eat within an hour or so before bed, and avoid caffeine and chocolate several hours before bed.

Alcohol can seriously affect your memory and concentration ability in several specific ways. Being intoxicated has been proven to negatively affect abstract thinking skills in people for at least 6 weeks! Alcohol affects sleep by contributing to sleep apnea, and many people who drink only moderately have been shown to sleep poorly. Regular use of alcohol contributes to weight gain and raises blood pressure. Limiting or stopping alcohol use entirely will assist you in many ways concerning the Court Officer vetting process.

Motivate yourself. Find a way to be enthusiastic in your preparation. Prove to yourself that you can earn a high score and make the grade. Keep a positive outlook and make it a fun challenge.

Study:

Start early. Begin preparing as soon as the exam is announced.

Avoid last minute cramming. Cramming does not work, but refreshing your memory on the night before the exam does.

Give yourself enough time to complete each practice exam in a single seating, without interruptions. This will give you more confidence and provide you with a realistic expectation for the actual exam.

Develop careful reading habits. You must become an active reader. For example, rephrase each question in your own words to make sure you understand the question. Re-check your answers and make sure your choice correctly answers the question.

Don’t try to memorize practice questions, instead focus on the process of reading carefully and actively.

Concentrate on the sections of the exam you find most challenging. Budget your time to practice more difficult areas.

How to answer difficult questions and sections:

Keep a positive attitude and outlook. Practicing questions in advance gives you confidence and experience in approaching hard questions.

Read difficult questions carefully. Make sure you know what is being asked. Then mentally restate it in your own words. Once you are sure of what is being asked, then proceed.

If you must, move on to another question and return if you have time. Be very careful, though, not to get out of order with bubbling in the answer sheet.

NEVER, <u>EVER</u> LEAVE ANY ANSWER BLANK.

Keep your test booklet and answer sheet close together, This helps ensure that your answer numbers match your question numbers.

If you skip a question and wish to return later, put a light mark in the test booklet next to the question (erase the marks later).

Don’t darken your answer space too heavily. It wastes time just darkening the space, and can cause a scanning error on the question if it does not erase well enough.

This exam is designed to penalize folks who are not prepared and practiced in particular types of questions, or who do not read carefully and make careless errors. By practicing, you will learn to read carefully and accurately and you will become proficient at the exact types of questions presented.

The Night Before

Briefly study and review the practice examination questions you have already completed. Focus on your successful responses. Your goal is to refresh your memory and reduce anxiety.

Re-Read your Admission Notice to confirm where the written examination will be held and what time it starts. Use Google Maps to print out a map. Check some online traffic sites to see if there is any unusual road work, etc. If you are using public transportation, check online to confirm that service is uninterrupted.

Organize the following in one place: Admission Notice; two forms of identification- one must be a photo ID such as a driver's license or passport; several sharp No. 2 pencils; and a watch.

The Day Of...

Plan to arrive at least 30 minutes before the scheduled time. Take into consideration that parking may be very difficult. Many of these exams are at public schools that may not have off-street parking. If this is the case, locate a parking garage in advance just in case you cannot find parking. Bring extra cash.

You should not risk bringing your phone into the exam. Consider securing it in your car or at home.

Though you cannot eat in the room, you can bring a snack to have just before entering the room. I recommend nuts and dried fruit, as they help balance and slowly raise blood sugar. Be sure to eat a hearty, but moderate meal in the morning. You want to be satisfied but not sleepy.

Use only No. 2 pencils to make your marks. I recommend bringing several sharp pencils, as they dull quickly. Frequently change them, and use a clean eraser for each correction. This way, there are no smudged marks that could cause a scanning error.

Do not be shy about asking your monitor for assistance. Also, feel free to politely ask the proctor to be quiet if they are talking or being disruptive.

During the Examination

Keep a positive outlook and remain optimistic. Try to see the test as a puzzle to be solved.

If you feel anxious, take a minute to close your eyes and focus on breathing carefully and deliberately. Visualize yourself in a comfortable place. Using a few placed "time outs" can make the experience much less stressful. (Obviously be aware of your timing here).

Remember to carefully read the directions before each part of the written exam. Each section of the exam has its own directions for you to read and follow.

Budget your time. The time allotted for each section of the exam is printed on the exam booklet. Time yourself with your watch so that you don't run out of time before completing the section. **Never Leave a Question Blank.**

Read each question or problem carefully. Read each possible answer choice before selecting your answer. If necessary, re-read the question until you have made sure you understand what is being asked.

Regularly check back to make sure you are putting your answer next to the right number on the answer sheet. If you need to skip a question leave a light mark next to the question so you may return later.

Before You Hand In Your Exam:

Double check all answers, check the order of your question responses on the scan sheet, and proofread wordy questions to make sure you answered each one correctly. Don't make changes unless you discover you clearly made a mistake and are certain about the answer. Make sure the answer sheet is carefully bubbled in, that there are no stray marks, and **No Blank Answers**. Check that there is only one bubble filled for each question.

Immediately after the exam:

As soon as you finish, find a quiet space to sit down and record your thoughts and impressions about the exam. Write down as many specific things as you can. This will help you, should you desire to take a similar exam for a different law enforcement title. This exam is very similar in format and difficulty to other exams you may later take. Recording your thoughts will assist you in developing an even better study plan for future exams

Chapter 3 Types of Questions on the exam

Remembering Facts and Information

You are given a written description of an event or incident involving court officers in or around a courthouse and are given five minutes to read and study the description before it is removed. You are then asked questions about the facts involved in the event or incident. The questions are very specific, frequently asking about names, dates, and locations. Using all 5 minutes to actively read is the key to success in this section.

Reading, Understanding and Interpreting Written Material

These questions measure how well candidates understand what they have read. There are two types of questions:

Format A (Reading Comprehension) You are given a brief reading selection followed by questions regarding the selection. All of the information required to answer the questions is provided in the selection. You are not required to have any special knowledge relating to the content area covered in the selections, though many of the selections are about courts and Court Officers.

Format B (Missing Word Selection) You are provided with short written passages from which words have been removed. You must select among four choices the word that most appropriately completes the passage.

Applying Facts and Information to Given Situations

These questions test your ability to take information which you have read and apply this information to a specific situation defined by a given set of facts. Each question contains a brief paragraph that describes a regulation, policy, or procedure which must be applied to a particular situation. All of the information needed to answer the questions is contained in the paragraph and in the description of the situation.

Clerical Checking

These questions measure a your ability to distinguish between sets of names, numbers, letters and/or codes which are almost exactly alike. Material usually is presented in three columns, and you are required to compare the information in the three sets.

Court Record Keeping

These questions measure a your ability to read, combine, and use written information organized from several places. You are given different tables which contain names, index numbers, addresses and other information, and must combine and reorganize the information to answer specific questions.

Chapter 4, "Remembering Facts and Information"

This type of question is quite common on many law enforcement civil service exams. It requires you to read a passage, usually about 300-350 words, for 5 minutes. The proctors then instruct you to put the passage away, and you are given a set of 5 or so questions to answer completely from memory. The questions are very specific in nature, and many candidates who do well have trained in reading deliberately and practiced memory exercises.

In preparing this book, I gave example questions to readers of all different educational backgrounds, had them read the paragraph for 5 minutes, and administered a question set. What I found is as follows:

Most readers read through the passage in 1-1 ½ minutes. Many then read through it a second time, and said "I'm Done". They felt that they had gotten the information. When I administered the question set, they all admitted that they were not prepared to answer such specific questions. They had not read it carefully or thoroughly.

The first lesson from this study was that a candidate must use all of the time given. Five minutes is a long time, and when used carefully, a candidate can read through the passage 3 or more times.

Second, A watch is necessary to help the reader pace the timing.

Third, the most successful candidates used visualization strategies and ordering to help remember various details and events.

Try to imagine yourself in the place you are reading about, (most likely a courthouse) As you read details, make mental pictures placing you in the scene you are reading about.

If an incident in the reading takes place on the 3rd floor of a courthouse, visualize looking at a 3 story building. Make a mental image of what it looks like.

If a day of the week is given, such as Tuesday, think of

something you do only on Tuesdays, or think of a song with that day in the title such as "Ruby Tuesday".

If a name is given, think of somebody you know with that name, or of a famous person who shares that name.

If times are given, try to order the events from earliest to latest- then recall them in order.

After reading the material the first time, look away briefly and mentally test yourself on the details. Ask yourself the "who", "what", "when", and "where" for details in the reading. Train yourself to recall, a paragraph at a time, the details.

As you can see, it is active brain work to remember and visualize all of these details. Train yourself to use up every second of reading time. You want to over-learn this material to the point of mastery.

Let's try a practice question set:

I. Remembering Facts and Information

You are provided with a written description of an event or incident and given a five (5) minute period to read and study the written description, after which it is removed. You will be instructed to not make any written notes about the event or incident. When you receive your test question booklet you will then be asked a series of questions about the facts involved in the event or incident.

Directions: Read the brief story below. Study it for five minutes. Then, turn the story over and answer the five questions on the following page.

A small coffee shop is located just south of the escalator on the ground floor of the Hamilton County Court House. In addition to coffee and newspapers, the shop sells buns, cookies, candy, chips, soda, and assorted fruits. In the mornings between 7:00 and 11:00 A.M., donuts and bagels also are available. Employees of the court and county workers often purchase items there. People also stop to ask directions because the building directory is located at the main entrance to the Court House, which is on the other side of the building.

The coffee shop is open daily from 7:00 A.M. to 5:00 P.M. It is operated by Frank James, who is 42 years old, has brown hair, brown eyes, and a thick build. His cousin, Mary Mercer, is a single mother and helps out part time.

On the morning of Wednesday, March 2, 2005 at about 9:15 A.M., Court Officer Stanley Jones stopped at the stand to purchase a bottle of water. While he was getting his water, a young man came up and asked where to find a Notary Public. He told him to take the elevator to the second floor and then turn right at the water fountain. While he was giving the directions, he noticed that Ms. Mercer was attempting to open a box of Swedish Fish candy with a box cutter.

The box cutter slipped and cut a laceration about 4 centimeters long in her right hand.

The court officer covered the wound with a sterile dressing from the first aid box, and Ms. Miller was taken to St. John's Hospital. She received fourteen stitches. Ms. Mercer did not return to work at the coffee shop for two weeks.

Examination Questions: Remembering Facts and Information

1. Who covered the wound with the sterile dressing?

A. Stanley Jones

B. Mary Mercer

C. Frank James

D. Marion Mueller

2. On what day of the week did the incident occur?

A. Monday

B. Tuesday

C. Wednesday

D. Friday

3. The name of the hospital was

A. St. James

B. St. Johns

C. St. Alban's

D. St. Anne's

4. The Notary Public is located

A. On the 2nd floor

B. On the 3rd floor

C. On the 4th floor

D. On the 5th floor

5. What hours is the newspaper stand open?

A. 7:00 A.M. to 2:00 P.M.

B. 7:00 A.M. to 5:00 P.M.

C. 7:00 A.M. to 10:00 A.M.

D. 7:00 A.M. to 4:00 P.M.

Solution

(1. A, 2. C, 3. B, 4. A, 5. B)

Chapter 5. Reading, Understanding and Interpreting Written Material. Format A, Reading Comprehension

This section of the written exam measures your ability to read and understand written material.

Questions on this test measure how well you understand what you have read. Each question contains a short reading selection. Following the selection is a set of questions pertaining to the information in the selection. All of the information required to answer the question(s) is given, so no prior knowledge about the topic is necessary. Remember, answer the questions based only on the information you read in the selection. Do not include your own knowledge in your responses.

Directions: After reading the selection below, choose the alternative which best answers the question following the selection.

The person in custody must, prior to interrogation, be clearly informed that he has the right to remain silent, and that anything he says will be used against him in court; he must be clearly informed that he has the right to consult with a lawyer and to have the lawyer with him during interrogation, and that, if he is indigent, a lawyer will be appointed to represent him.

-Justice Earl Warren, Miranda vs. Arizona.

1. Which one of the following best describes what must happen before a person in custody is interrogated?

A. He must remain silent.

B. He must be clearly informed of his right to remain silent.

C. He must use an attorney.

D. An attorney will be freely assigned to him in all circumstances.

Solution

Answer B. You do not need any knowledge about the law to answer this question. All the information is in the paragraph. Answer A is not correct because nowhere does it state the person in custody must remain silent.. Answer C is incorrect because the paragraph states he has a right to use an attorney, not an obligation to use one. Answer D is incorrect because an attorney will only be appointed to indigent people.

6. Reading, Understanding and Interpreting Written Material:

Format B (Missing Word Selection)

Questions on this portion of the test measure how well you can fit words into a passage to create a meaningful sentence.

Each part of this section contains a short, written passage from which some words have been omitted. You need to select one word from the four choices that best fits each blank space.

Directions: The passage below contains five numbered blanks. Read the passage once quickly to get the overall idea of the passage. Read it a second time, this time thinking of words that might fit in the blanks. Below the passage are listed sets of words numbered to match the blanks. Pick the word from each set which seems to make the most sense both in the sentence and the total paragraph.

The Secretary of State___(1)___ the county clerk of the county ___(2)___ which the commission of a notary public is filed may certify to the official character of ___(3)___ notary public and any notary public may file his autograph signature and a certificate of official character in the office of ___(4)___ county clerk of any county in the ___(5)___ and in any register's office in any county having a register and thereafter such county clerk may certify as to the official character of such notary public.

Question 1	Question 2	Question 3	Question 4	Question 5
A. that	A. in	A. all	A. any	A. State
B. of	B. at	B. many	B. all	B. town
C. your	C. for	C. such	C. none	C. village
D. or	D. to	D. all	D. neither	D. hamlet

Solutions (1.D, 2.A, 3.C, 4.A, 5 A)

7. Applying Facts and Information to Given Situations

This section of the written exam measures your ability to take information which you have read and apply it to a specific situation defined by a given set of facts. Each question contains a paragraph which describes a regulation, procedure or law. The selection is followed by a description of a specific situation. Then a question is asked which requires you to apply the law, regulation, or procedure described in the paragraph to the specific situation. Remember that all of the information you need to answer the question is contained in the paragraph and in the description of the situation. You need to read and understand both before you attempt to answer the question. Do not use your own knowledge here. Stick to the policy how it is written.

Directions: Use the information proceeding each question to answer the question. Only that information should be used in answering the questions. Do not use any prior knowledge you may have on the subject. Choose the alternative that best answers the question.

Effective November 3, 2004, employees who are entitled to be paid at an overtime minimum wage rate according to the terms of a New York State minimum wage order must be paid for overtime at a rate at least one and a half times the appropriate regular minimum wage rate for non-overtime work. For the purpose of this policy statement, the term "appropriate regular minimum wage rate" means $7.75 per hour or a lower minimum wage rate established in accordance with the provisions of a New York State minimum wage order. OVERTIME MINIMUM WAGES MAY NOT BE OFFSET BY PAYMENTS IN EXCESS OF THE REGULAR MINIMUM RATE FOR NON-OVERTIME WORK.

1. A worker who ordinarily works forty hours a week at an agreed wage of $8.00 an hour is required to work fifty hours during a payroll week and is paid for the extra ten hours at a rate of $9.50 per hour rate. Using the information contained in the above passage, it is best to conclude:
A. the employee was underpaid
B. the employee was not underpaid
C. the employee was not underpaid because he or she agreed upon the wage rate
D. the employee should find another job is he is dissatisfied

2. According to the information in the above passage, the employee in Question 1 was most likely underpaid at least:
A. $60.00
B. $40.00
C. $25.00
D. not underpaid at all

Solutions

1. (A) The employee was underpaid. The extra pay should have added $40.00, but the employee was only paid $15.00 in overtime.

2. (C) The employee was only paid $15.00 in overtime when he should have been paid $40.00. The difference in pay was $25.00.

8. Clerical Checking

This section of the examination measures your ability to determine whether different sets of words, numbers, names and codes are similar. No matter what the form of the item, you are required to scan the sets of information, identify where the sets differ, and use the directions to determine the correct answer.

Directions: Questions 1 & 2

The following two questions, numbered 1 and 2, consist of three sets of information.

Compare the information in the three sets presented in each question. On your answer sheet, mark:

Choice A: if all three sets are exactly alike

Choice B: if only the first and third sets are exactly alike

Choice C: if only the first and second sets are exactly alike

Choice D: if none of the sets are exactly alike.

Question 1. (Note: In this format the information is on the same line in each set.)

ISBN0652319134	ISBN0652319134	ISBN0652319134
Jones, Harmon	Jones, Harmon	Jones, Harmon
Hospital and Care	Hospital & Care	Hospital and Care
Doctor's Print Co.	Doctor's Print Co.	Doctor's Print Co.
FG3831.H391999	FG3831.H391999	FG3831.H391999

Question 2. (Note: In this format the information is not on the same line in each set.)

Googan, Marina	KF387.D39	Penal Law
Penal Law	Googan, Marina	New York: Pressman
New York: Pressman	Penal Law	KF387.D39
KF387.D39	New York: Pressman	Googan, Marina

Solution- Question 1.

Answer B. The "and" in the third line of the second set was typed "&" but the first and third sets contain exactly the same information; therefore the correct answer is B.

Solution - Question 2.

Answer A. The information in each of these sets is the same, even though the order of the information is on different lines in each set.

9. Record Keeping

On the following pages is a simplified version of the type of record keeping exercise that will be included in the written examination. The Record Keeping test on the written examination that you will take will have different types of tables and information. The purpose of this example is to show you how a Record Keeping test might look so that you can be better prepared to answer the questions in this section of the written examination.

Directions: Answer the four questions based on the information contained in the following tables. Remember, all of the information needed to answer the questions correctly can be found in the tables. Hint: Sometimes it pays to complete the "Daily Breakdown of Cases" and "Summary of Cases" tables before you attempt to answer any of the questions, but sometimes it is not necessary. Check the questions first so that you don't waste time and risk errors from reading the additional chart.

Daily Log of Cases Thursday			
Judge	Date Filed	Status	Money Award
Stone	11/06/11	Adjourned	X
Harper	11/30/11	Adjourned	X
Bigs	02/10/13	Dismissed	X
Evans	06/28/12	Dismissed	X
Bigs	08/23/11	Dismissed	X

Daily Log of Cases Friday			
Judge	Date Filed	Status	Money Award
O'toole	07/14/11	Settled	$1,595
Evans	07/09/12	Settled	$11,400
Bigs	07/15/13	Dismissed	X
Stone	06/30/12	Dismissed	X
Evans	10/01/11	Defaulted	X
O'toole	06/09/11	Adjourned	X
Stone	07/17/12	Settled	$760
Bigs	09/23/11	Settled	X

Daily Breakdown of Cases (Thursday and Friday)			
Case Status	Thursday	Friday	Total Cases
Dismissed			
Adjourned			
Defaulted			
Settled- No Money Award			
Settled- Money Award			
Total Cases			
Cases Filed By Year			
2011			
2012			
2013			
Total Cases			

Summary of Cases (Thursday and Friday)

Judge	Status			Settled No Money Award	Settled Money Award	Total Cases
	Dismissed	Adjourned	Defaulted			
Stone						
O'toole						
Evans						
Harper						
Bigs						

1. What was the total number of adjourned cases on Friday?

A. 2 B. 3 C.1 D. 0

2. How many settled cases on Thursday and Friday had money awards of more than $2,000?

A. 0 B. 1 C. 2 D. 3

3. How many cases before Judge Stone on Thursday and Friday were dismissed?

A. 0 B. 1 C. 2 D. 3

4. Which judge had the largest settlement?

A. Evans B. Stone C. Harper D. O'toole

Solutions:

1. Answer C. You could have answered this question by counting up all the cases in Friday's "Daily Log of Cases" that said "Adjourned" in the "Status" column. Alternatively, you could have looked in your completed "Daily Breakdown of Cases" table under "Friday" and across from "Adjourned."

2. Answer B. To answer this question you need to refer directly to Friday's "Daily Log of Cases." Since money awards are only made for settled cases, you need to look only in the "Money Award" column and count the number of times an award of more than $2,000 appears.

3. Answer B. The easiest way to answer this question is to refer to your completed "Summary of Cases" table which includes cases from Thursday and Friday. Look across the name from "Stone" and down the column marked "Dismissed."

4. Answer A. Evans had the largest settlement at $11,400.

Practice Exam I

Try to set aside enough time to complete this practice exam in one sitting. Two hours should allow you enough time to complete the exam and review your responses.

I. Remembering Facts and Information

You are provided with a written description of an event or incident and given a five (5) minute period to read and study the written description, after which it is removed. You will be instructed to not make any written notes about the event or incident. When you receive your test question booklet you will then be asked a series of questions about the facts involved in the event or incident.

Directions: Read the brief story below. Study it for five minutes. Then, turn the story over and answer the five questions on the following page.

The Dutchess County Supreme Court House is located on Hamilton St. in Poughkeepsie, NY. There are three wings, a lobby and five floors. There are four court parts, Parts A-D. Court Officer Francis James is one of the eleven officers assigned to this courthouse, along with one Sergeant and one Lieutenant. There are generally two officers in each part and three on patrol.

Officer James's hours are from 7:00 A.M. to 4:00 P.M. It is her 7th year as a Court Officer and her 3rd at that location. Her first assignment was in the Supreme Court Building in Bronx County. She hopes to one day be reassigned to Westchester County, which is closer to her home.

On Friday, February 6, 2009 Court Officer James is on patrol in the first-floor hallway. At approximately 10:15 A.M., Lieutenant Mary Richards walks up to her and tells her that she needs her help in Part B, Judge Robert Parker's part. When Court Officer James enters the courtroom, she sees two witnesses engaged in an altercation. One woman, Ms. Lilly Peters, has her hands on the other woman's head and appears to be pulling her hair. Lieutenant Richards grabs Ms. Peters from behind, while Officer James takes charge of the other.

Lieutenant Richards then places Ms. Peters under arrest. Officer James asks the other witness, Ms. Lisa Roberts, if she needs any assistance and she refuses. The officer then gives

Ms. Peters a summons for disorderly conduct.

Lieutenant Richards takes Ms. Peters to a holding cell and returns to the courtroom. She thanks

Officer James for her help, commends her on her actions and instructs her to complete the appropriate paperwork. She completes the form, turns it in to the Sergeant for review, and clocks out at 4:15 P.M.

Questions about the story on the next page ....

Examination Questions: Remembering Facts and Information

1. What are Court Officer Johnson's hours?

A. 7:00 A.M. to 4:00 P.M.

B. 11:00 A.M. to 5:00 P.M.

C. 7:00 A.M. to 5:30 P.M.

D. 11:00 A.M. to 5:30 P.M.

2. The incident takes place in what county?

A. Westchester

B. Dutchess

C. Rockland

D. Bronx

3. What is the name of the woman who was being attacked?

A. Richards

B. Blake

C. Roberts

D. James

4. How many court parts are there in this court?

A. Two

B. Four

C. Five

D. Twelve

5. Who took the woman to the holding cell?

A. The Sergeant

B. Court Officer Johnson

C. The Lieutenant

D. Court Officer James

II. Reading, Understanding and Interpreting Written Material

This section of the written exam measures your ability to read and understand written material.

There are two formats contained in the test which are used to measure your reading ability. You should familiarize yourself with each of the formats used in the test.

Format A

In this format, each question contains a brief reading selection followed by a question or questions pertaining to the information in the selection. All of the information required to answer the question(s) is provided, so even if the reading selection is on a topic with which you are not familiar, you will be able to answer the question(s) by reading the selection carefully.

Remember, answer the questions based only on the information you read in the selection.

Directions: After reading the selection below, choose the alternative which best answers the question following the selection.

Set1

The County Clerk generally forwards all mail to the judge in his or her county. But, the addresses of Supreme Court Clerks are also included for your convenience. If you are unsure of the Supreme Court address, always send your mail to the County Clerk, who will forward it to the appropriate party.

If you already have an index number, you should send your documentation to the Supreme Court Clerk and should include the index number with all correspondence. If you do not have an index number and you are filing a new petition (like an Article 52 petition), you need to file a Request for Judicial Intervention ("RJI") with the County Clerk to obtain an index number. When mailing documentation, you should make specific reference to the person you are trying to contact.

1. Based on the above passage, which of the following statements is most accurate?

A. It is the county Clerk's responsibility to forward all mail to the Judge in his or her county.

B. County Clerks should read all of the Judge's mail.

C. County Clerks may respond on behalf of a judge.

D. A Clerk must return all mail not sent directly to a specific Judge.

2. According to the passage, Why is the address of the Supreme Court Clerk provided?

A. It makes things easier for the Clerk

B. For the convenience of the County Clerk

C. For the convenience of the reader

D. to expedite the filing of the documents

3. If you are unsure of the Supreme Court address, always

A. send it to the postmaster

B. hire a courier

C. send it return receipt

D. send it to the County Clerk

4. If you are filing an Article 52 petition and you do not have an index number you must

A. send it return receipt

B. request an "RJI" from the County Clerk

C. make reference to the person you are trying to contact

D. use your Social Security number

5. If you have an index number, to whom should you send your documentation to?

A. Supreme Court Clerk

B. Notary Public

C. County Clerk

D. Any Court Officer on duty

Set 2

After commencement of an action wherein e-filing is authorized, documents may be electronically filed and served, but only by, and electronic service shall be made only upon, a party or parties who have consented thereto. A party's failure to consent to participation in electronic filing and service shall not bar any other party to the action from filing documents electronically with the County Clerk and the court or serving documents upon any other party who has consented to participation. A party who has not consented to participation shall file documents with the court and the County Clerk, and serve and be served with documents, in hard copy. When an e-filing party serves a document in hard copy on a non-participating party, the document served shall bear full signatures of all signatories and proof of such service shall be filed electronically.

1. What must happen before e-filing a document?
A. The document must be notarized
B. e-filing must be authorized
C. Electronic service must be cancelled
D. All parties must be served hard copies first

2. When may a party file documents with the County Clerk electronically?
A. Only when all parties have agreed
B. Only when the County Clerk allows
C. Whenever the party chooses
D. When all parties demonstrate access to computers

3. How must a party be served papers who has not consented to electronic service?
A. Electronically, if the County Clerk allows
B. Electronically
C. In hard copy
D. through the newspaper

4. How is proof of service filed by an e-filing party who has served papers on a party who has not consented to e-filing?
A. In person in the Clerk's Office
B. Via courier
C. Through the mail
D. Electronically

II. Reading, Understanding and Interpreting Written Material

Format B

In this format the test contains a short, written passage from which some words have been omitted. You need to select one word from the four alternatives that best completes the passage.

Directions: The passages below each contain five numbered blanks. Read the passage once to get the overall idea of the passage. Read it a second time, this time thinking of words that might fit in the blanks. Below the passage are listed sets of words numbered to match the blanks. Pick the word from each set which seems to make the most sense both in the sentence and the total paragraph.

Set 1

The world is (1) different now. For man holds (2) his mortal hands the power to (3) all forms of human poverty and all forms of human life. And yet the same revolutionary (4) for which our forebears fought are still at issue around the globe — the belief that the rights of man come not (5) the generosity of the state, but from the hand of God.

John F. Kennedy's Inaugural Address

Question 1	Question 2	Question 3	Question 4	Question 5
A. that	A. at	A. abolish	A. beliefs	A. where
B. another	B. for	B. tell	B. kind	B. from
C. very	C. in	C. believe	C. reason	C. whether
D. a	D. behind	D. suggest	D. offer	D. with

Set 2

When in the Course of human events (1) becomes necessary for one people to dissolve the political bands which have connected them (2) another and to assume (3) the powers of the earth, the separate and equal station to which the (4) of Nature and of Nature's God entitle them, a decent respect to the opinions (5) mankind requires that they should declare the causes which impel them to the separation.

- Declaration of Independence

Question 1	Question 2	Question 3	Question 4	Question 5
A. that	A. at	A. abolish	A. beliefs	A. of
B. another	B. with	B. among	B. Laws	B. from
C. it	C. in	C. believe	C. reason	C. whether
D. a	D. behind	D. suggest	D. offer	D. with

III. Applying Facts and Information to Given Situations

This section of the written exam measures your ability to take information which you have read and apply it to a specific situation defined by a given set of facts. Each question contains a brief paragraph which describes a regulation, procedure or law. The selection is followed by a description of a specific situation. Then a question is asked which requires you to apply the law, regulation, or procedure described in the paragraph to the specific situation. Remember that all of the information you need to answer the question is contained in the paragraph and in the description of the situation. You need to read and understand both before you attempt to answer the question.

Directions: Use the information preceding each question to answer the question. Only that information should be used in answering the questions. Do not use any prior knowledge you may have on the subject. Choose the alternative that best answers the question.

RULE: As a Court Officer you must always:

1. Obey all lawful orders of your superiors.
2. Remain on your assigned post until properly relieved.
3. Refrain from unnecessary talking with other court employees or the public while on duty.
4. Refer all requests for information from the media to your supervisor.
5. Report any unusual situations or problems to your supervisor.

SITUATION 1: During a recess of a criminal trial to which you are assigned, a man approaches you in the hallway outside the courtroom. He identifies himself as a reporter for one of the local newspapers and shows his press credentials. He says he has heard a rumor that the victims father is attending the trial today and asks you to confirm or deny this.

Based solely on the above Rule and Situation, which one of the following is your most appropriate response to the reporter?

A. Refer the request to your supervisor.
B. Deny the rumor, even though it is true.
C. State firmly and clearly “No Comment”.
D. Instruct him to leave the premises.

SITUATION 2: While at your assigned post, another court officer approaches you and begins making small talk about recent sporting events and cracking jokes. You are aware that your assignment is a security detail, and that you are in full view of the public. How should you respond?

A. Tell the Court officer to “shut up”
B. Remind the Court Officer to refrain from unnecessary talking while on duty, then remain silent.
C. Continue with the banter as it increases friendships and creates a relaxed environment.
D. Ignore the Officer.

IV. Clerical Checking

This section of the examination measures your ability to determine whether different sets of words, numbers, names and codes are similar. No matter what the form of the item, you are required to scan the sets of information, identify where the sets differ, and use the directions to determine the correct answer.

Directions:

The following three questions, consist of three sets of information.

Compare the information in the three sets presented in each question. On your answer sheet, mark:

Choice A: if all three sets are exactly alike

Choice B: if only the first and third sets are exactly alike

Choice C: if only the first and second sets are exactly alike

Choice D: if none of the sets are exactly alike.

Question 1. (Note: In this format the information is on the same line in each set.)

223738292013	222738292013	223738282013
Family Court	Family Court	Family Court
Joel Curiaas	Joel Curiaas	Joel Curias
Robbery I	Robbery I	Robbery I

Question 2. (Note: In this format the information is not on the same line in each set.)

Cummings, Richard 5480 Main St. White Plains, NY`(914) 655-5590
Cummings, Richard 5480 Main St. White Plains, NY (914) 655-4590
Cummings, Richard 5480 Main St. White Plains, NY (914) 655-5590

Question 3. (Note: In this format the information is not on the same line in each set.)

Dirk, James	351 104th St.	Jamaica, NY 11624	(718)334-2423
(718)334-2424	351 104th St.	Dirk, James	Jamaica, NY 11624
(718)334-2424	Dirk, James	351 104th St.	Jamaica, NY 11624

Question 4. (Note: In this format the information is not on the same line in each set.)

Sharon Gonzalez	Sharon Gonzalez	Sharon Gonzalez
54 Laird Drive	54 Laird Drive	54 Laird Drive
Hartford, NY 13413	Hartford, NJ 13413	Hartford, NY 13413
160-40-6973	160-40-6973	160-40-6973
47.75 hrs. @ $9.05/hr.	47.75 hrs. @ $9.05/hr.	47.75 hrs. @ $9.05/hr.
9/3/90 - 10/9/91	9/3/90 - 10/9/91	9/3/90 - 10/9/91
$88.50	$88.50	$58.50

V. Record Keeping

Directions: Answer the four questions based on the information contained in the following tables. Remember, all of the information needed to answer the questions correctly can be found in the tables. Complete the "Daily Breakdown of Cases" and

"Summary of Cases" tables before you attempt to answer any of the questions.

Daily Log of Cases Thursday			
Judge	Date	Status	Money Award
Arthur	04/08/13	Adjourned	X
Chester	11/16/12	Adjourned	X
James	03/12/12	Settled	$2104
Everett	03/12/13	Adjourned	X
James	04/23/11	Dismissed	X
James	11/11/11	Adjourned	X
Arthur	03/05/13	Dismissed	X
Everett	03/10/13	Settled	$13,555

Daily Log of Cases Friday			
Judge	Date Filed	Status	Money Award
Davis	05/13/12	Settled	X
Everett	05/12/11	Settled	$11,400
James	04/06/13	Settled	$15,444
Arthur	06/22/13	Dismissed	X
Everett	11/05/12	Defaulted	X
Davis	06/21/13	Adjourned	X
Arthur	08/18/12	Settled	$760
James	09/02/11	Settled	X
Davis	05/15/12	Settled	$1917
Arthur	06/21/12	Adjourned	X
Chester	06/22/13	Settled	$2200

Daily Breakdown of Cases (Thursday and Friday)			
Case Status	Thursday	Friday	Total Cases
Dismissed			
Adjourned			
Defaulted			
Settled- No Money Award			
Settled- Money Award			
Total Cases			
Cases Filed By Year			
2011			
2012			
2013			
Total Cases			

Summary of Cases (Thursday and Friday)

Judge	Status Dismissed	Adjourned	Defaulted	Settled No Money Award	Settled Money Award	Total Cases
Arthur						
Davis						
Everett						
Chester						
Rawlins						
James						

Questions

1. What was the total number of Settled cases on Thursday?

A. 2 B. 3 C. 5 D. 8

2. How many settled cases on Thursday and Friday, for which there was a monetary award, was the award less than $5,000?

A. 0 B. 1 C. 2, D. 4

3. How many cases before Judge James on Thursday and were dismissed?

A. 0 B. 1 C. 2 D. 3

4. Which Judge had the largest settlements?

A. Arthur B. Davis C. Chester D. James

Practice Examination 1, Solutions

Part I Remembering Facts and Information

(1. A, 2. B, 3. C, 4. B, 5. C)

Part II, Format A

Set 1
(1.A, 2.C, 3.D, 4.B, 5.A)

Set2
(1. B, 2. C, 3. C, 4.D)

Part II, Format B
Set 1(1.C, 2.C, 3.A, 4.A, 5.B)

Set2 (1.C, 2.B, 3.B, 4.B, 5.A)

Part III Applying Facts and Information To Given Situations

Situation 1

Correct answer is A

Situation 2

Correct answer is B

Part IV Clerical Checking

(1. A, 2.B, 3. D, 4.D)

Part V. Record Keeping

(1.A, 2. D, 3. B, 4. D)

Practice Exam II

I. Remembering Facts and Information

You are provided with a written description of an event or incident and given a five (5) minute period to read and study the written description, after which it is removed. You will be instructed to not make any written notes about the event or incident. When you receive your test question booklet you will then be asked a series of questions about the facts involved in the event or incident.

Directions: Read the brief story below. Study it for five minutes. Then, turn the story over and answer the five questions on the following page.

The Kings County Family Court House is located on 333 Jay Street, Brooklyn NY. There are three wings, a main lobby and five floors. There are seven court parts, Parts A-G. Court Officer Marcus Jeffries is one of the 16 officers assigned to this courthouse, along with one Sergeant and one Lieutenant. There are generally two officers in each part and two on patrol.

Officer Jeffries' hours are from 7:00 A.M. to 4:00 P.M. It is his 7th year as a Court Officer and his 4th at that location. His prior assignment was in the Family Court Building in Queens County. He hopes to one day be reassigned to Nassau County, which is closer to his daughter's school.

On Friday, March 19, 2013 Court Officer Jeffries' is on patrol in the 3rd floor, North Wing. At approximately 9:45 A.M., Lieutenant Jessica Northrup walks up to him and tells him that she needs his help in Part C, Judge Margot Parker's part. When Court Officer Jeffries enters the courtroom, he sees a man and his former wife, Rebecca Horn engaged in an altercation. The man, Rev. Martin Wright, has his hands blocking his face while the woman appears to be punching him. Lieutenant Northrup grabs the woman from behind, while Officer Jeffries takes charge of Rev. Wright.

Lieutenant Northrup then places Rebecca Horn under arrest. Officer Jeffries asks Rev. Wright if he needs any assistance and he requests first aid for a contusion to his head and an ambulance. The officer then gives Ms. Horn a summons for disorderly conduct.

Lieutenant Northrup takes Ms. Horn to a holding cell and returns to the courtroom. She thanks Officer Jeffries for his help, commends him on his actions and instructs him to complete the appropriate paperwork. He completes the form, turns it in to the Lieutenant for review, and clocks out at 5:30 P.M.

Questions about the story on the next page ....

Examination Questions: Remembering Facts and Information

1. What are Court Officer Jeffries' hours?

A. 7:00 A.M. to 4:00 P.M.

B. 11:00 A.M. to 5:00 P.M.

C. 8:00 A.M. to 5:30 P.M.

D. 11:00 A.M. to 5:30 P.M.

2. The incident takes place in what county?

A. Richmond

B. Orange

C. Kings

D. Nassau

3. What is the name of the man who was being attacked?

A. Parkinson

B. Blake

C. Wright

D. Anderson

4. How many court parts are there in this court?

A. Two

B. Four

C. Seven

D. Twelve

5. Who took the man to the holding cell?

A. The Sergeant

B. Court Officer Johnson

C. The Lieutenant

D. Court Officer Miles

II. Reading, Understanding and Interpreting Written Material

This section of the written exam measures your ability to read and understand written material.

There are two ways or formats contained in the test which are used to measure your reading ability. You should familiarize yourself with each of the formats used in the test.

Format A

In this format, each question contains a brief reading selection followed by a question or questions pertaining to the information in the selection. All of the information required to answer the question(s) is provided, so even if the reading selection is on a topic with which you are not familiar, you will be able to answer the question(s) by reading the selection carefully.

Remember, answer the questions based only on the information you read in the selection.

Directions: After reading the selection below, choose the alternative which best answers the question following the selection.

The increasing demands upon our highways from a growing population and the development of forms of transportation not anticipated when the highways were first built have brought about congestion, confusion, and conflict, until the yearly toll of traffic accidents is now at an appalling level. If the death and disaster that traffic accidents bring throughout the year were concentrated into one calamity, we would shudder at the tremendous catastrophe. The loss is no less catastrophic because it is spread out over time and space.

1. Which one of the following statements concerning the yearly toll of traffic accidents is best supported by the passage above?

A. It is increasing the demands for safer means of transportation.

B. It has resulted in increased congestion, confusion, and conflict on our highways.

C. It does not shock us as much as it should because the accidents do not all occur together.

D. It has resulted mainly from the new forms of transportation.

2. According to the passage, what is putting an increased demand on highways?

A. Maintenance costs

B. growing population

C. aging infrastructure

D. accidents

3. According to the passage, what is the result of the increasing demands put on our highways?

A. potholes

B. higher costs

C. higher population

D. congestion, confusion, and conflict

II. Reading, Understanding and Interpreting Written Material

(Continued)

Format B

In this format the test contains a short, written passage from which some words have been omitted. You need to select one word from the four alternatives that best completes the passage.

Directions: The passage below contains five numbered blanks. Read the passage once quickly to get the overall idea of the passage. Read it a second time, this time thinking of words that might fit in the blanks. Below the passage are listed sets of words numbered to match the blanks. Pick the word from each set which seems to make the most sense both in the sentence and the total paragraph.

"Upon the faith of these acknowledgments rests the title ___(1)___ real property, ___(2)___ the only security to ___(3)___ titles is the fidelity with which notaries and commissioners of deeds perform their duty in requiring the appearance of parties to such instruments ___(4)___ them and always refusing to execute a certificate unless the parties are actually known to them or the identity of the ___(5)___ executing the instruments is satisfactorily proved."

Question 1	Question 2	Question 3	Question 4	Question 5
A. that	A. and	A. all	A. before	A. parties
B. of	B. at	B. many	B. all	B. exchange
C. your	C. for	C. such	C. none	C. documents
D. or	D. to	D. all	D. neither	D. instrument

III. Applying Facts and Information to Given Situations

This section of the written exam measures your ability to take information which you have read and apply it to a specific situation defined by a given set of facts. Each question contains a brief paragraph which describes a regulation, procedure or law. The selection is followed by a description of a specific situation. Then a question is asked which requires you to apply the law, regulation, or procedure described in the paragraph to the specific situation. Remember that all of the information you need to answer the question is contained in the paragraph and in the description of the situation. You need to read and understand both before you attempt to answer the question.

Directions: Use the information preceding each question to answer the question. Only that information should be used in answering the questions. Do not use any prior knowledge you may have on the subject. Choose the alternative that best answers the question.

Manual workers must be paid weekly and not later than seven calendar days after the end of the week in which the wages are earned. However, a manual worker employed by a non-profit making organization must be paid in accordance with the agreed terms of employment, but not less frequently than semimonthly. A manual worker means a mechanic, workingman or laborer. Railroad workers, other than executives, must be paid on or before Thursday of each week the wages earned during the seven-day period ending on Tuesday of the preceding week. Commission sales-personnel must be paid in accordance with the agreed terms of employment but not less frequently than once in each month and not later than the last day of the month following the month in which the money is earned. If the monthly payment of wages, salary, drawing account or commissions is substantial, then additional compensation such as incentive earnings may be paid less frequently than once in each month, but in no event later than the time provided in the employment agreement.

Questions:

1. A non-executive railroad worker has not been paid for the previous week's work. It is Wednesday.
According to the above passage, which of the following is true?
a. the above regulation was not violated, since the ending period is the following Tuesday
b. the above regulation was violated
c. the above regulation was not violated, since the employee could be paid on Thursday
d. the above regulation does not apply in this case

2. What type of worker is not covered by this rule?
A. railroad executives
B. mechanic
C. laborer
D. workingman

3. What worker would be considered a "manual" worker?
A. Executive
B. Contract Accountant
C. Office supervisor
D. laborer

IV. Clerical Checking

This section of the examination measures your ability to determine whether different sets of words, numbers, names and codes are similar. No matter what the form of the item, you are required to scan the sets of information, identify where the sets differ, and use the directions to determine the correct answer.

Directions:

The following questions consist of three sets of information.

Compare the information in the three sets presented in each question. On your answer sheet, mark:

Choice A: if all three sets are exactly alike

Choice B: if only the first and third sets are exactly alike

Choice C: if only the first and second sets are exactly alike

Choice D: if none of the sets are exactly alike.

1. (Note: In this format the information is on the same line in each set.)

Fruchter, Michael	Fruchter, Michael	Fruchter, Michael
543 East Avenue	543 East Avenue	543 East Avenue
Leeds, N.Y. 12435	Leeds, N.Y. 12435	Leeds, N.Y. 12345
817-43-4537	817-43-4537	817-43-4537
5' 10" 170 lbs. GR	5' 10" 170 lbs. GR	5' 10" 170 lbs. GR
K743251796534	K743251796534	K743251796534
XT4D375YR	XT4D375YR	XT4D375YR

2.(Note: In this format the information is on the same line in each set.)

James, Joyce
234 Sycamore
S. Garden City, NY
212-51-1323
5'2" 120 lbs. Br
N2013-023759CV
MVL2220.2323

James, Joyce
234 Sycamore
S. Garden City, NY
212-51-1323
5'2" 120 lbs. Br
N2013-023759CV
MVL2220.2323

James, Joyce
234 Sycamore
S. Garden City, NY
212-51-1323
5'2" 120 lbs. Br
N2013-023759CV
MVL2220.2323

3. (Note: In this format the information is not on the same line in each set.)

Jones, Carltton
104-33-2123
Brooklyn, NY 11213
464 W. 23rd. ave.

464 W. 23rd ave.
Jones, Carlton
104-33-3123
Brooklyn, NY 11121

Brooklyn, NY 11212
464 W. 23rd st.
Jones, Carllton
104-33-3233

V. Record Keeping

Directions: Answer the five questions based on the information contained in the following tables. Remember, all of the information needed to answer the questions correctly can be found in the tables. Complete the "Daily Breakdown of Cases" and "Summary of Cases" tables before you attempt to answer any of the questions.

Daily Log of Cases Monday			
Judge	Date	Status	Money Award
Sullivan	11/08/14	Adjourned	X
Baker	11/15/14	Adjourned	X
Tredwell	02/12/12	Dismissed	X
Tepher	03/27/13	Adjourned	X
Zuma	08/23/13	Dismissed	X
Sullivan	02/12/12	Adjourned	X
Baker	02/03/13	Settled	$14,500
Tepher	01/04/12	Settled	$2250
Zuma	07/30/13	Dismissed	X
Zuma	02/21/12	Adjourned	X

Daily Log of Cases Wednesday			
Judge	Date Filed	Status	Money Award
Shine	12/13/13	Adjourned	X
Sullivan	05/06/12	Settled	$14,400
Baker	01/05/09	Settled	$25,422
Tepher	05/17/14	Dismissed	X
Zuma	11/12/13	Defaulted	X
Tredwell	05/15/14	Settled	X
Sullivan	07/06/13	Settled	$2751
Tredwell	08/20/12	Settled	X

Daily Breakdown of Cases (Monday and Wednesday)			
Case Status	Thursday	Friday	Total Cases
Dismissed			
Adjourned			
Defaulted			
Settled- No Money Award			
Settled- Money Award			
Total Cases			
Cases Filed By Year			
2012			
2013			
20014			
Total Cases			

Summary of Cases (Thursday and Friday)

Judge	Status Dismissed	Adjourned	Defaulted	Settled No Money Award	Settled Money Award	Total Cases
Shine						
Sullivan						
Baker						
Tredwell						
Tepher						
Zuma						

Question 1. What was the total number of adjourned cases on Monday?

A. 2 B. 3 C. 5 D. 8

Question 2. How many settled cases on Monday and Wednesday, for which there was a monetary award, was the award less than $5,000?

A. 0 B. 1 C. 2 D. 3

Question 3. How many cases before Judge Zuma on Monday and Wednesday were adjourned?

A. 0 B. 1 C. 2 D. 3

4. What was the highest settlement award?

A. $25,422 B. $87,200 C. $14,400 D. $6700

5. Which Judge had the greatest number of adjournments?

A. Baker B. Sullivan C. Shine D. Zuma

Solutions

Part I Remembering Facts and Information

Answers can be found in the Memory Story. (1. A, 2. C, 3. C, 4. C, 5. C)

Part II, Format A

1. C, 2. B, 3.D

Part II, Format

(1.B, 2.A, 3.C, 4.A, 5 A)

Part III, Applying Facts and Information to Given Situations

1. C, 2. A, 3. D

Part IV, Clerical Checking

1. C, 2. A, 3. D

Record Keeping Part V:

1. C, 2. C, 3. B, 4. A, 5. A

Practice Exam III

I. Remembering Facts and Information

You are provided with a written description of an event or incident and given a five (5) minute period to read and study the written description, after which it is removed. You will be instructed to not make any written notes about the event or incident. When you receive your test question booklet you will then be asked a series of questions about the facts involved in the event or incident.

Directions: Read the brief story below. Study it for five minutes. Then, turn the story over and answer the five questions on the following page.

The Montgomery County Civil Court House is a distinctive, Modern Classic of a building, built between 1938 and 1940. It was built with local funds combined with a grant from the Federal WPA. Mayor Stinson laid the cornerstone in 1938, and presided over the building's dedication on October 22, 1940. The new courthouse consolidated various court facilities in downtown Leonia. It originally housed the offices of the Montgomery County Clerk, the City Court, the Supreme Court and the Surrogate's Court. It was meant to handle all the civil cases in Montgomery County.

The Classical style of the building was chosen as it expressed the power and majesty of the law. A classic example of the style, the E shaped seven-story building is faced with Arkansas limestone and is ornamented with neo-classical features. Its most prominent feature is a tall colonnaded entrance fronted by a grand staircase. At the center of the building the three entrances retain their original bronze doors and are edged with bronze panels depicting famous lawgivers. Other notable features include the heavy bracketed cornices, balustrade balconies, stylized swagged relief panels, and shallow window surrounds.

Architects Alfred H. Elias and William W. Golden were Montgomery County residents with architectural practices in

Steuben who had designed a number of important Southern Tier buildings. In 1940, just before it opened, the building was awarded first prize as one of the Best Buildings of the Year in New York State. The building's carefully constructed and designed facades, beautiful details, and the power of its imposing entrance make it one of finest and most awe inspiring public buildings in Montgomery County.

Today, the building houses the Montgomery County Civil Court as well as the County Clerk's Office. Its hours are 8:30-5:00 Monday through Friday. Criminal Court cases are tried and weddings are conducted in Marvin Gardens.

Questions about the story on the next page ....

Examination Questions: Remembering Facts and Information

1. What hours is the Montgomery County Civil Court House open?

A. 8:30 A.M. to 5:00 P.M.

B. 11:00 A.M. to 5:00 P.M.

C. 8:00 A.M. to 5:30 P.M.

D. 11:00 A.M. to 5:30 P.M.

2. Where are weddings conducted?

A. Kew Gardens

B. Forest Hills

C. Marvin Gardens

D. Leonia

3. What is the name of one of the building's architects?

A. Parkington

B. Blake

C. Golds

D. Elias

4. How many floors are there in this courthouse?

A. Two

B. Four

C. Seven

D. Twelve

5. What year did the building open?

A. 1937

B. 1938

C. 1939

D. 1940

II. Reading, Understanding and Interpreting Written Material

This section of the written exam measures your ability to read and understand written material.

There are two formats contained in the test which are used to measure your reading ability. You should familiarize yourself with each of the formats used in the test.

Format A

In this format, each question contains a brief reading selection followed by a question or questions pertaining to the information in the selection. All of the information required to answer the question(s) is provided, so even if the reading selection is on a topic with which you are not familiar, you will be able to answer the question(s) by reading the selection carefully.

Remember, answer the questions based only on the information you read in the selection.

Directions: After reading the selection below, choose the alternative which best answers the question following the selection.

The Secretary of State or the county clerk of the county in which the commission of a notary public is filed may certify to the official character of such notary public and any notary public may file his autograph signature and a certificate of official character in the office of any county clerk of any county in the State and in any register's office in any county having a register and thereafter such county clerk may certify as to the official character of such notary public.

1. Based on the passage, which of the following statements is most accurate?

A. A Notary Public may certify the official character of the County Clerk.
B. The Secretary of state is the only person who may certify the official character of a Notary Public.
C. Both the Secretary of State or the County Clerk may certify the official character of a Notary Public..
D. A Notary Public must file their certificate in any county they sign in.

2. According to the passage, where is the Certificate of Official Character filed?
A. Secretary of State
B. County Court
C. Town Clerk
D. County Clerk

II. Reading, Understanding and Interpreting Written Material, Format B

In this format the test contains a short, written passage from which some words have been omitted. You need to select one word from the four alternatives that best completes the passage.

Directions: The passage below contains five numbered blanks. Read the passage once to get the overall idea of the passage. Read it a second time, this time thinking of words that might fit in the blanks. Below the passage are listed sets of words numbered to match the blanks. Pick the word from each set which seems to make the most sense both in the sentence and the total paragraph.

Set 1

In any prosecution ___(1)___ larceny based upon a false promise, the defendant's intention ___(2)___ belief that the promise would ___(3)___ be performed may not be established by or inferred from the fact alone that such promise was not performed. Such a finding may be based only ___(4)___ evidence establishing that the facts and circumstances of the case are wholly consistent with guilty intent or belief and wholly inconsistent with innocent intent or belief, and ___(5)___ to a moral certainty every hypothesis except that of the defendant's intention or belief that the promise would not be performed;

Question 1	Question 2	Question 3	Question 4	Question 5
A. that	A. or	A. all	A. before	A. parties
B. for	B. at	B. many	B. all	B. exchange
C. your	C. for	C. such	C. upon	C. excluding
D. or	D. to	D. not	D. neither	D. instrument

Set 2

In any prosecution ___(1)___ larceny based upon a false promise, the defendant's intention ___(2)___ belief that the promise would ___(3)___ be performed may not be established by or inferred from the fact alone that such promise was not performed. Such a finding may be based only ___(4)___ evidence establishing that the facts and circumstances of the case are wholly consistent with guilty intent or belief and wholly inconsistent with innocent intent or belief, and ___(5)___ to a moral certainty every hypothesis except that of the defendant's intention or belief that the promise would not be performed;

Question 1	Question 2	Question 3	Question 4	Question 5
A. that	A. or	A. all	A. before	A. parties
B. for	B. at	B. many	B. all	B. exchange
C. your	C. for	C. such	C. upon	C. excluding
D. or	D. to	D. not	D. neither	D. instrument

III. Applying Facts and Information to Given Situations Set I

This section of the written exam measures your ability to take information which you have read and apply it to a specific situation defined by a given set of facts. Each question contains a brief paragraph which describes a regulation, procedure or law. The selection is followed by a description of a specific situation. Then a question is asked which requires you to apply the law, regulation, or procedure described in the paragraph to the specific situation. Remember that all of the information you need to answer the question is contained in the paragraph and in the description of the situation. You need to read and understand both before you attempt to answer the question.

Directions: Use the information preceding each question to answer the question. Only that information should be used in answering the questions. Do not use any prior knowledge you may have on the subject. Choose the alternative that best answers the question.

One of the duties of Human Resources is processing employee requests for leaves of absence. When an employee requests a leave of absence, HR's responsibility is to advise the employee regarding his or her benefit coverage. Each type of leave is associated with its own benefit coverage, as shown in the guidelines below.
A. Educational Leave of Absence
1. Employee must prepay 80% of medical insurance for the term of the leave.
2. Employee must prepay 90% of dental insurance for the term of the leave.
B. Personal Leave of Absence
1. Employee must pay 75% of medical costs on a monthly basis.
2. Employee must pay 100% of dental costs on a monthly basis.

1. Which of the following describes the medical payment obligation for an employee's personal leave of absence?
A) 75% of costs on a monthly basis
B) 80% of insurance for the term of the leave
C) 90% of insurance for the term of the leave
D) 100% of costs on a monthly basis

2. What percentage of medical insurance does the employer pay for an Educational Leave of Absence?
A. 25%
B. 20%
C. 30%
D. 50%

3. What percentage of dental costs must an employee pay out on a Personal Leave of Absence?
A. 0%
B. 20%
C. 50%
D. 100%

III. Applying Facts and Information to Given Situations Set II

Departmental policy requires that all employees follow these guidelines for display of items in the Officer Locker Room.
*Items for display must not be larger than 10" by 12".
*Items may not be displayed in hallways or restrooms.
*Items for display on the inside of locker can be of a non-confidential business or personal nature.
*Items for display on the bulletin board may only be work-related material.
*Items for display on the outside walls on main corridors need to be approved by a supervisor.
*Items posted anywhere in the facility may not be of an offensive, sarcastic, or sexual nature.

1. You are involved in a charity group outside of work that has asked you to display a 10 by 13 inch flyer asking for donations. Where can you display the flyer?
A) Restroom
B) Entrance hallway
C) Outside module wall
D) Cannot be displayed

2. You cut out a newspaper article about upcoming musical events to your area. The size of the article is 6 by 9 inches.
Where can you display the article?
A) In your locker
B) Inside locker room only
C) Outside locker room wall only
D) Cannot be displayed

3. You just received a new Snap-on calendar featuring tools, cars, and women in lingerie. The calendar measures 8" x 8". Where can it be displayed?
A) In the restroom.
B) In your locker
C) Nowhere in the facility
D) On the bulletin board

IV. Clerical Checking

IV. Clerical Checking

This section of the examination measures your ability to determine whether different sets of words, numbers, names and codes are similar. No matter what the form of the item, you are required to scan the sets of information, identify where the sets differ, and use the directions to determine the correct answer.

Directions: The following two questions consist of three sets of information. Compare the information in the three sets presented in each question. On your answer sheet, mark:

Choice A: if all three sets are exactly alike

Choice B: if only the first and third sets are exactly alike

Choice C: if only the first and second sets are exactly alike

Choice D: if none of the sets are exactly alike.

1. (Note: In this format the information is on the same line in each set.)

234738292014	234738292014	234738282014
Family Court	Family Court	Family Court
Martin Smyth	Martin Smythe	Martin Smyth
Robbery I	Robbery I	Robbery I

2. (Note: In this format the information is on the same line in each set.)

ISBN0952319369	ISBN0952319369	ISBN0652319369
Henry, Patrick	Henry, Patrick	Henry, Patrick
Property Law	Property Law	Property Law
Law Journal	Law Journal	Law Journal
KF3821.H391972	KF3821.H391972	KF3821.H391972

3. (Note: In this format the information is not on the same line in each set.)

2013CV213829	Ruphus Jones	Brooklyn Supreme
Ruphus Jones	Brooklyn Supreme	2013CV213829
104-22-3434	2013CV213829	104-23-3434
Brooklyn Family	104-23-3434	Rupus Jones

V. Record Keeping

Directions: Answer the five questions based on the information contained in the following tables. Remember, all of the information needed to answer the questions correctly can be found in the tables. Complete the "Daily Breakdown of Cases" and

"Summary of Cases" tables before you attempt to answer any of the questions.

Daily Log of Cases Tuesday			
Judge	Date	Status	Money Award
Brick	11/08/11	Settled	$22,000
Cunis	11/15/12	Adjourned	X
Davis	02/12/12	Dismissed	X
Edgar	03/27/13	Adjourned	X
Formosa	08/23/13	Dismissed	X
Cunis	02/21/12	Settled	$19,500
Brick	01/12/12	Settled	$13,122
Formosa	11/12/13	Settled	$775

Daily Log of Cases Friday			
Judge	Date Filed	Status	Money Award
Formosa	07/13/12	Settled	$6,999
Evans	12/09/11	Settled	$11,400
Brick	5/06/12	Settled	$15,444
Davis	07/27/12	Dismissed	X
Davis	09/05/11	Defaulted	X
Formosa	06/11/13	Adjourned	X
Edgar	10/18/11	Settled	$760
Edgar	10/24/12	Settled	$2121

Daily Breakdown of Cases (Tuesday and Friday)			
Case Status	Tuesday	Friday	Total Cases
Dismissed			
Adjourned			
Defaulted			
Settled- No Money Award			
Settled- Money Award			
Total Cases			
Cases Filed By Year			
2011			
2012			
2013			
Total Cases			

Summary of Cases (Tuesday and Friday)

Judge	Status			Settled No Money Award	Settled Money Award	Total Cases
	Dismissed Adjourned Defaulted					
Brick						
Cunis						
Davis						
Edgar						
Formosa						

1. What was the total number of adjourned cases on Tuesday?
A. 2 B. 3 C. 5 D. 8

2. How many settled cases on Tuesday and Friday, for which there was a monetary award, was the award less than $5,000?
A. 0 B. 1 C. 2, D. 3

3. How many cases before Judge Davis on Tuesday and Friday were dismissed?
A. 0 B. 1 C. 2 D. 3

4. Which judge had the highest settlement?
A. Davis B. Formosa C. Edgar D. Brick

5. Which Judge had the most dismissed cases?
A. Brick B. Davis C. Formosa D. Cunis

Solution

I. Remembering Facts and Information

(1. A, 2. C, 3. D, 4. C, 5. D)

II. (Format A). Reading, Understanding and Interpreting Written Material; Reading Comprehension

(1.C, 2.D)

II. (Format B). Reading, Understanding and Interpreting Written Material; Word Matching

Set 1 (1. B, 2. A, 3. D, 4. C, 5. C)

Set 2 (1. B, 2. A, 3. D, 4. C, 5. C)

III. Applying Facts and Information to Given Situations, Set I

(1. A, 2.B, 3.D)

III. Applying Facts and Information to Given Situations, Set I

(1. D, 2. D, 3. C)

IV. Clerical Checking

(1. D, 2. C, 3. D)

V. Record Keeping

(1.A, 2.D, 3.C, 4. D, 5. B)

Appendix

The Coat of Arms of The State of New York, "Excelsior"

The coat of arms of the State of New York was formally adopted in 1778, and appears at the center of the State's flag and seal.

The shield displays a three-masted ship and a sloop on the Hudson River, bordered by a green shoreline and a mountain range in the background with the sun rising behind it.

There are two women, each standing on one side of the shield: On the left is Liberty, with the imagery of a Phrygian cap (A Roman symbol for the pursuit of liberty and freedom) raised on a pole. Her left foot stands upon a crown that represents freedom from the British monarchy that once ruled the colony of New York. On the right is Justice, wearing a blindfold (representing impartiality) and holding scales (representing fairness) and a sword (representing the will to protect and enforce Justice).

A banner below the shield shows the motto Excelsior, meaning "higher", translated as "Ever Upward."

The shield is surmounted by a crest consisting of an eagle standing on a world globe.

The flag of the State of New York is the coat of arms on a solid blue background. The state seal of New York is the coat of arms surrounded by the words "The Great Seal of the State of New York."

Civil Court Structure

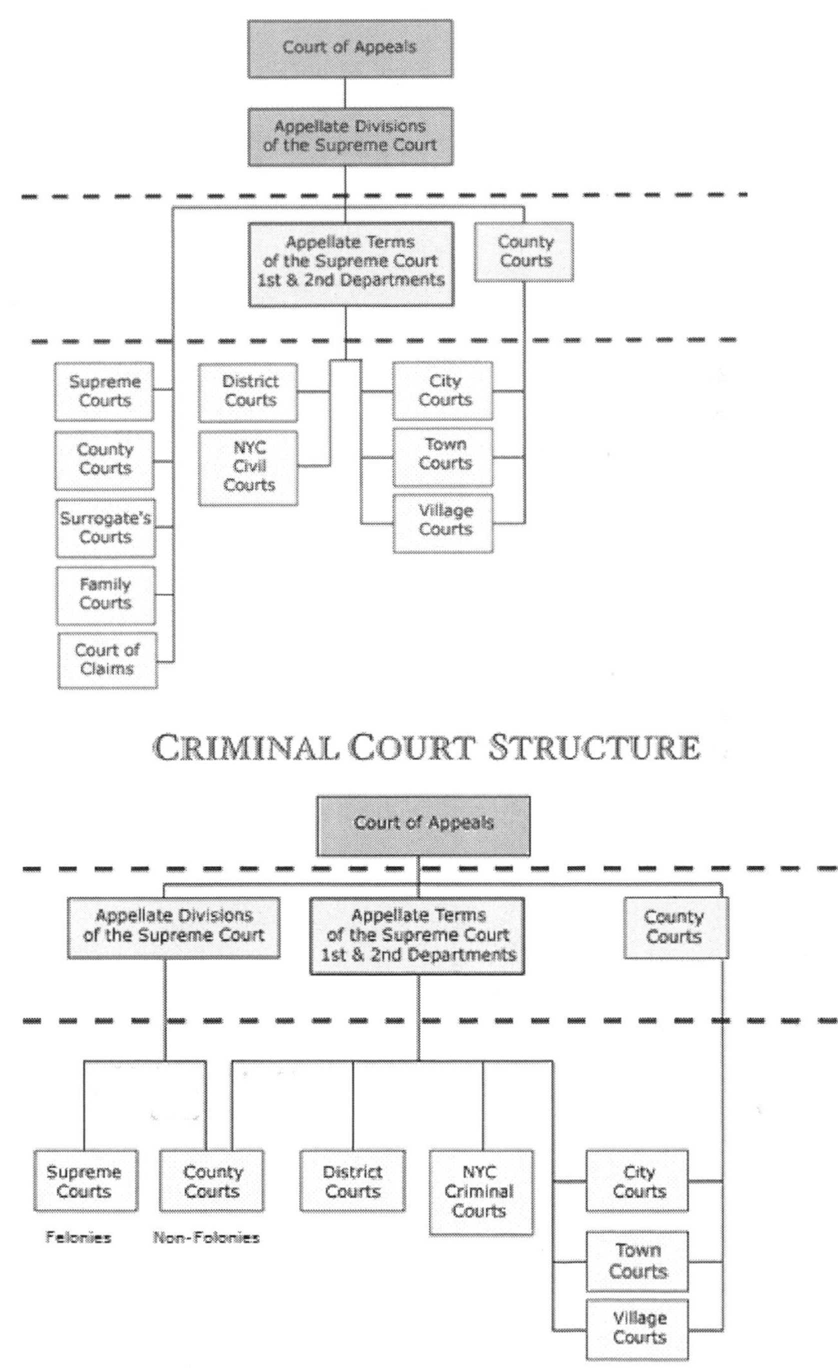

Chain of Command; Rank

Though Not at all necessary to do well on the Court Officer exam, it is interesting to learn a little bit about the Rank structure of the Court Officers. Below is a table showing the various ranks currently in use.

Chain of Command for Court Officers	**Insignia**
Chief of the Department of Public Safety	4 Gold Stars
First Deputy Chief of the Department of Public Safety	3 Gold Stars
Deputy Chief of the Department of Public Safety	2 Gold Stars
Assistant Chief of the Department of Public Safety	1 Gold Star
New York State Court Officer - Major	Golden Oak Leaf
New York State Court Officer - Captain	Two Gold Bars
New York State Court Officer - Lieutenant	One Gold Bar
New York State Court Officer – Sergeant	3 Stripes
New York State Senior Court Officer	
New York State Court Officer	
New York State Court Officer - Trainee	

Glossary

Though all questions on the exam can be answered without knowing legal terminology, it may prove helpful to read through some of these terms to raise your familiarity with the courts as a whole.

ACLU- American Civil Liberties Union. An organization whose mission is "to defend and preserve the individual rights and liberties guaranteed to every person in this country by thc Constitution and laws of the United States."

ADA- Abbreviation for Assistant District Attorney

Arraignment- A court hearing where a formal reading of criminal charges against the defendant to inform the defendant of the charges against him or her. In response, the defendant is expected to enter a plea.

Arrest- An arrest means taking someone into custody, against their will, in order to prosecute or question. It involves a physical force, or submission to an officer's show of force, and the person arrested is not free to leave.

Bail- Money that is deposited with a court to persuade it to release a suspect from jail, on the grounds that the suspect will return for trial or forfeit the bail. Bail funds may be returned at the end of the trial, if all court appearances are made.

Court Clerk- A court clerk is an officer of the court whose responsibilities include maintaining the records of a court. Another duty is to administer oaths to witnesses, jurors, and grand jurors. The clerk is also the custodian of the court's seal, which is used to authenticate copies of the court's orders, judgments and other records.

Civil Case- A type of case where one party sues another.

Corporation Council- the title given to a legal officer in some US municipal and county jurisdictions, who handles civil claims against the city, including negotiating settlements and defending the municipality when it is sued. In New York City, the corporation council also prosecutes some juvenile delinquency cases.

Court Officer- A sworn Peace Officer who is charged with the safety and security of the NYS Unified Court System.

Criminal Case- A type of case where a person is formally charged with a crime and tried in front of a jury of their peers. Different classes of crimes include felonies and misdemeanors.

Grand Jury- A grand jury in New York State is a body of 16-23 people that is empowered to investigate potential criminal conduct and to determine whether criminal charges should be brought. If the Jury decides there is evidence to hold a trial, a formal incitement is handed down.

Defendant- The party in court who is either defending against criminal or civil charges, ie. the person who is being charged or sued.

District Attorney- A lawyer employed by the government who investigates and prosecutes criminal cases on behalf of the people of the community.

Executed- to be signed.

Index Number- A Unique number assigned to each case by the Court Clerk. Numbers are sequential and restart each year in each court.

Legal Aid Society- The oldest and largest provider of legal services to the poor people. It operates both traditional civil and criminal law cases.

Part- a court room where specified business of a court is to be conducted by a judicial officer.

Peace Officer-The powers of Peace Officers in New York State are stated in Article 2 of the Consolidated Laws of Criminal Procedure. The major difference between Peace and Police officers in New York involves the writing and executing of warrants.

Plaintiff- The party in court who is pressing a case or suing in court.

Public Defender- A lawyer provided by the court to serve as counsel for people who cannot afford their own attorney.

Sequester- to remove or withdraw a jury into solitude or seclusion. This action, though rarely taken, is meant to protect the jury from influence, intimidation, or tampering.

Stenographer/ Court Reporter- A court employee who records court proceedings in the form of a written transcript.

Subscribed- To be written.

Transcript- The written proceedings of a court hearing or trial.

Witnessed- When an incident or occurrence has been viewed by someone.

For a more comprehensive glossary of legal terms visit: http://www.nycourts.gov/lawlibraries/glossary.shtml#A

ABOUT THE AUTHOR

Seth S. Patton has written numerous Civil Service Exam Titles. He has a BS and MS in Secondary Education from SUNY New Paltz and a MS in Educational Administration from Touro College. His graduate work focused on Educational Assessment and testing development.

He has written exam items for the New York State Education Department.

He enjoys studying for, taking, writing and teaching about civil service exams.

Made in the USA
Lexington, KY
11 August 2014